LOOK FOR THE GOOD

Hi! These pages are about to become a delight! Here you will create a habit to think positively and look for the good around you! Each day record what has made your day a little sweeter! Was it something you did? Smelled? Saw? Ate? Maybe it was a feeling you had?
Draw a picture, write it down, or both!

Additional weekly ideas of how to add sweetness to those around you!

My Spoonfuls of Sugar

_____

This journal belongs to someone sweet!

SPOONFULS OF SUGAR

Smile at someone.

"If you see someone without a smile, give them one of yours."
-Dolly Parton

Date:

Today was sweet because...

_____
_____
_____

Date:

Today was sweet because...

Date:

Today was sweet because...

SPOONFULS OF SUGAR

Date:

Today was sweet because...

Date:

Today was sweet because...

Date:

Today was sweet because...

Date:

Today was sweet because...

SPOONFULS OF SUGAR

Wave to a neighbor! You will make their day!

"Kindness is the language which the deaf can hear and the blind can see."
-Mark Twain

Date:

Today was sweet because...

Date:

Today was sweet because...

Date:

Today was sweet because...

SPOONFULS OF SUGAR

Date:

> Today was sweet because...

Date:

> Today was sweet because...

Date:

> Today was sweet because...

Date:

> Today was sweet because...

SPOONFULS OF SUGAR

Call a relative. Ask them about their day.

Date:

Today was sweet because...

_____
_____
_____

Date:

Today was sweet because...

_____
_____
_____

Date:

Today was sweet because...

_____
_____
_____

SPOONFULS OF SUGAR

Date:

Today was sweet because...

_____
_____
_____

Date:

Today was sweet because...

_____
_____
_____

Date:

Today was sweet because...

Date:

Today was sweet because...

_____
_____
_____

SPOONFULS OF SUGAR

Draw a picture for a friend and put it in their mailbox!

Date:

Today was sweet because...

_____
_____
_____

Date:

Today was sweet because...

_____
_____
_____

Date:

Today was sweet because...

_____
_____
_____

SPOONFULS OF SUGAR

Date:

Today was sweet because...

Date:

Today was sweet because...

Date:

Today was sweet because...

Date:

Today was sweet because...

SPOONFULS OF SUGAR

Give a tight hug, then squeeze even tighter!

Date:

Today was sweet because…

Date:

Today was sweet because…

Date:

Today was sweet because…

SPOONFULS OF SUGAR

Date:

Today was sweet because...

_____
_____
_____

Date:

Today was sweet because...

_____
_____
_____

Date:

Today was sweet because...

_____
_____

Date:

Today was sweet because...

_____
_____

SPOONFULS OF SUGAR

Give a high-five to someone.
Up high and down low!

"Give people high fives just for getting out of bed. Being a person is hard sometimes."
-Kid President

Date:

Today was sweet because...

Date:

Today was sweet because...

Date:

Today was sweet because...

SPOONFULS OF SUGAR

Date:

Today was sweet because...

_____
_____
_____

Date:

Today was sweet because...

_____
_____
_____

Date:

Today was sweet because...

_____
_____
_____

Date:

Today was sweet because...

_____
_____
_____

SPOONFULS OF SUGAR

Put your dishes in the sink after eating.
*OR put them in the dishwasher!

"Wash the plate not because it is dirty nor because you are told to wash it, but because you love the person who will use it next."
-St. Teresa of Calcutta

Date:

Today was sweet because...

_____
_____
_____

Date:

Today was sweet because...

Date:

Today was sweet because...

_____
_____

SPOONFULS OF SUGAR

Date:

Today was sweet because...

_____
_____
_____

Date:

Today was sweet because...

_____
_____
_____

Date:

Today was sweet because...

_____
_____
_____

Date:

Today was sweet because...

_____
_____
_____

SPOONFULS OF SUGAR

Look at pictures taken of you. You've done a lot of good things!

"Photography lets children learn who they are and where they fit."
-Judy Weiser

Date:

Today was sweet because...

Date:

Today was sweet because...

Date:

Today was sweet because...

SPOONFULS OF SUGAR

Date:

Today was sweet because...

_____
_____
_____

Date:

Today was sweet because...

_____
_____
_____

Date:

Today was sweet because...

Date:

Today was sweet because...

_____
_____
_____

SPOONFULS OF SUGAR

Create art on the sidewalk with chalk for others to see.

"Every child is an artist."
-Picasso

Date:

Today was sweet because...

Date:

Today was sweet because...

Date:

Today was sweet because...

SPOONFULS OF SUGAR

Date:

Today was sweet because...

_____
_____
_____

Date:

Today was sweet because...

_____
_____
_____

Date:

Today was sweet because...

_____
_____
_____

Date:

Today was sweet because...

_____
_____
_____

SPOONFULS OF SUGAR

Help set
the table
for a meal.

"In every job that must be done,
there is an element of fun. You find
the fun and snap! The job's a
game!"
-Mary Poppins

Date:

Today was sweet because...

_____

_____

_____

Date:

Today was sweet because...

Date:

Today was sweet because...

SPOONFULS OF SUGAR

Date:

Today was sweet because...

_____
_____
_____

Date:

Today was sweet because...

_____
_____
_____

Date:

Today was sweet because...

_____
_____

Date:

Today was sweet because...

_____
_____

SPOONFULS OF SUGAR

Learn a new joke and share it.

"The trick is to enjoy life. Don't wish away your days, waiting for better ones ahead."
-Marjorie Pay Hinckley

Date:

Today was sweet because...

Date:

Today was sweet because...

Date:

Today was sweet because...

SPOONFULS OF SUGAR

Date:

Today was sweet because...

_____
_____
_____

Date:

Today was sweet because...

_____
_____
_____

Date:

Today was sweet because...

_____
_____
_____

Date:

Today was sweet because...

_____
_____
_____

SPOONFULS OF SUGAR

Date:

Today was sweet because...

Mail a thank you picture or card.

"Gratitude paints little smiley faces on everything it touches."
-Richelle E. Goodrich

Date:

Today was sweet because...

Date:

Today was sweet because...

SPOONFULS OF SUGAR

Date:

Today was sweet because...

Date:

Today was sweet because...

Date:

Today was sweet because...

Date:

Today was sweet because...

SPOONFULS OF SUGAR

Make cookies with someone you love.

Date:

Today was sweet because...

Date:

Today was sweet because...

Date:

Today was sweet because...

SPOONFULS OF SUGAR

Date:

Today was sweet because...

_____
_____
_____

Date:

Today was sweet because...

_____
_____
_____

Date:

Today was sweet because...

Date:

Today was sweet because...

_____
_____
_____

SPOONFULS OF SUGAR

Date:

Share your favorite toy.

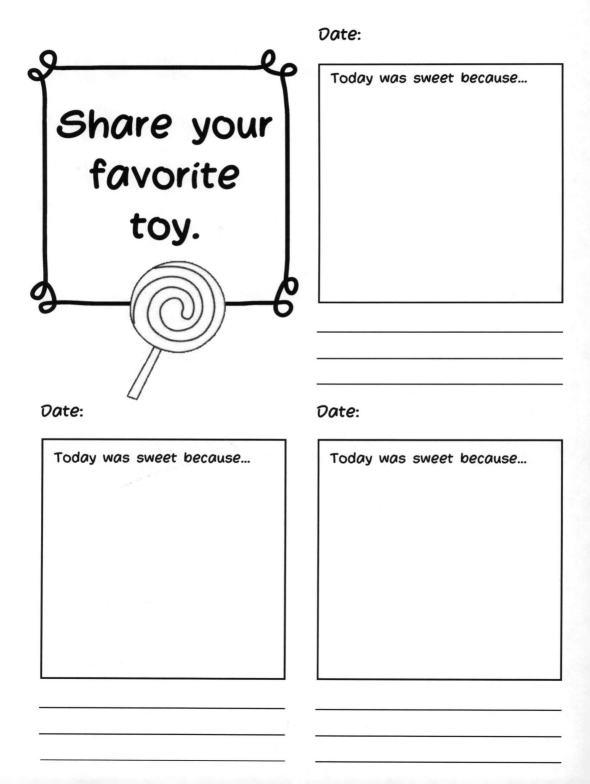

Today was sweet because...

_____
_____
_____

Date:

Today was sweet because...

_____
_____

Date:

Today was sweet because...

_____
_____

SPOONFULS OF SUGAR

Date:

Today was sweet because...

Date:

Today was sweet because...

Date:

Today was sweet because...

Date:

Today was sweet because...

SPOONFULS OF SUGAR

Let someone else have a turn first.

Date:

Today was sweet because...

_____
_____
_____

Date:

Today was sweet because...

_____
_____
_____

Date:

Today was sweet because...

_____
_____
_____

SPOONFULS OF SUGAR

Date:

Today was sweet because...

_____
_____
_____

Date:

Today was sweet because...

_____
_____
_____

Date:

Today was sweet because...

Date:

Today was sweet because...

_____
_____
_____

SPOONFULS OF SUGAR

Invite someone to try a new activity with you!

"Take chances, make mistakes, get messy!"
-Miss Frizzle

Date:

Today was sweet because...

Date:

Today was sweet because...

Date:

Today was sweet because...

SPOONFULS OF SUGAR

Date:

Today was sweet because...

_____
_____
_____

Date:

Today was sweet because...

_____
_____
_____

Date:

Today was sweet because...

_____
_____
_____

Date:

Today was sweet because...

_____
_____
_____

SPOONFULS OF SUGAR

Read a book
with
someone.
Enjoy each
page.

"You can find magic wherever you look. Sit back and relax, all you need is a book."
-Dr. Seuss

Date:

Today was sweet because...

_____
_____
_____

Date:

Today was sweet because...

Date:

Today was sweet because...

_____
_____

SPOONFULS OF SUGAR

Date:

Today was sweet because...

_____
_____
_____

Date:

Today was sweet because...

_____
_____
_____

Date:

Today was sweet because...

_____
_____

Date:

Today was sweet because...

_____
_____

SPOONFULS OF SUGAR

Shh
Secretly serve someone else who lives in your home.

"Happiness springs from doing good and helping others."
-Plato

Date:

Today was sweet because...

Date:

Today was sweet because...

Date:

Today was sweet because...

SPOONFULS OF SUGAR

Date:

Today was sweet because...

_____
_____
_____

Date:

Today was sweet because...

_____
_____
_____

Date:

Today was sweet because...

Date:

Today was sweet because...

_____
_____
_____

SPOONFULS OF SUGAR

Say,
"I love you" to
someone you
love.

"If you want to change
the world, go home and
love your family."
-Mother Teresa

Date:

Today was sweet because...

Date:

Today was sweet because...

Date:

Today was sweet because...

SPOONFULS OF SUGAR

Date:

Today was sweet because...

_____
_____
_____

Date:

Today was sweet because...

_____
_____
_____

Date:

Today was sweet because...

_____
_____
_____

Date:

Today was sweet because...

_____
_____
_____

SPOONFULS OF SUGAR

Go for a walk with a friend, talk about the nature you see. Birds. Trees. Clouds.

"The earth laughs in flowers."
-Ralph Waldo Emerson

Date:

Today was sweet because...

_____
_____
_____

Date:

Today was sweet because...

Date:

Today was sweet because...

_____
_____
_____

SPOONFULS OF SUGAR

Date:

Today was sweet because...

Date:

Today was sweet because...

Date:

Today was sweet because...

Date:

Today was sweet because...

SPOONFULS OF SUGAR

Dance to your favorite song. Keep dancing until someone joins you!

"Dancers create magic, so that makes [you] magical."
-Stephanie Lahart

Date:

Today was sweet because...

Date:

Today was sweet because...

Date:

Today was sweet because...

SPOONFULS OF SUGAR

Date:

> Today was sweet because...

Date:

> Today was sweet because...

Date:

> Today was sweet because...

Date:

> Today was sweet because...

SPOONFULS OF SUGAR

Give a nice compliment!

"Try to be a rainbow in someone's cloud."
-Maya Angelou

Date:

Today was sweet because...

Date:

Today was sweet because...

Date:

Today was sweet because...

SPOONFULS OF SUGAR

Date:

Today was sweet because...

Date:

Today was sweet because...

Date:

Today was sweet because...

Date:

Today was sweet because...

SPOONFULS OF SUGAR

Tell someone who teaches you, "Thank you!"

Date:

Today was sweet because...

Date:

Today was sweet because...

Date:

Today was sweet because...

SPOONFULS OF SUGAR

Date:

Today was sweet because...

_____
_____
_____

Date:

Today was sweet because...

_____
_____
_____

Date:

Today was sweet because...

Date:

Today was sweet because...

_____
_____

SPOONFULS OF SUGAR

Date:

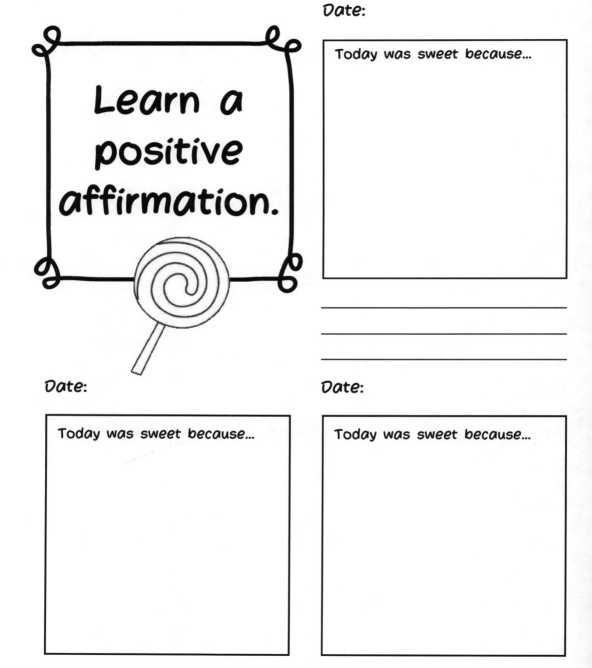

Learn a positive affirmation.

Today was sweet because...

_____
_____
_____

Date:

Today was sweet because...

_____
_____
_____

Date:

Today was sweet because...

_____
_____
_____

SPOONFULS OF SUGAR

Date:

Today was sweet because...

_____
_____
_____

Date:

Today was sweet because...

Date:

Today was sweet because...

_____
_____
_____

Date:

Today was sweet because...

_____
_____
_____

SPOONFULS OF SUGAR

Play a game with someone. Be a good sport. Cheer them on!

Date:

Today was sweet because...

_____
_____
_____

Date:

Today was sweet because...

_____
_____
_____

Date:

Today was sweet because...

_____
_____
_____

SPOONFULS OF SUGAR

Date:

Today was sweet because...

_____
_____
_____

Date:

Today was sweet because...

_____
_____
_____

Date:

Today was sweet because...

_____
_____
_____

Date:

Today was sweet because...

_____
_____
_____

SPOONFULS OF SUGAR

Share your "Spoonfuls of Sugar" with someone else.

"If you have good thoughts they will shine out of your face like sunbeams and you will always look lovely."
-Roald Dahl

Date:

Today was sweet because...

Date:

Today was sweet because...

Date:

Today was sweet because...

SPOONFULS OF SUGAR

Date:

Today was sweet because...

_____
_____
_____

Date:

Today was sweet because...

_____
_____
_____

Date:

Today was sweet because...

_____
_____
_____

Date:

Today was sweet because...

_____
_____
_____

SPOONFULS OF SUGAR

Help someone with a need.

"As you grow older, you will discover that you have two hands; one for helping yourself, the other for helping others."
-Audrey Hepburn

Date:

Today was sweet because...

Date:

Today was sweet because...

Date:

Today was sweet because...

SPOONFULS OF SUGAR

Date:

Today was sweet because...

_____
_____
_____

Date:

Today was sweet because...

_____
_____
_____

Date:

Today was sweet because...

_____
_____
_____

Date:

Today was sweet because...

_____
_____
_____

SPOONFULS OF SUGAR

Share with someone what makes you happy.

"It's a good day to have a good day."
-Bill Anderson

Date:

Today was sweet because...

Date:

Today was sweet because...

Date:

Today was sweet because...

SPOONFULS OF SUGAR

Date:

Today was sweet because...

_____
_____
_____

Date:

Today was sweet because...

_____
_____
_____

Date:

Today was sweet because...

Date:

Today was sweet because...

_____
_____
_____

SPOONFULS OF SUGAR

Make a funny face at someone! Wait until they laugh!

"There's power in looking silly and not caring that you do."
-Amy Poehler

Date:

Today was sweet because...

Date:

Today was sweet because...

Date:

Today was sweet because...

SPOONFULS OF SUGAR

Date:

Today was sweet because...

_____
_____
_____

Date:

Today was sweet because...

_____
_____
_____

Date:

Today was sweet because...

_____
_____
_____

Date:

Today was sweet because...

_____
_____
_____

SPOONFULS OF SUGAR

Who has a birthday this month? Wish them Happy Birthday!

"Every day of your life is a special occasion."
-Thomas S Monson

Date:

Today was sweet because...

_____
_____
_____

Date:

Today was sweet because...

Date:

Today was sweet because...

SPOONFULS OF SUGAR

Date:

Today was sweet because...

Date:

Today was sweet because...

Date:

Today was sweet because...

Date:

Today was sweet because...

SPOONFULS OF SUGAR

Bring a treat to a friend.

"Sometimes me think, what is friend? And then me say: a friend is someone to share last cookie with."
-Cookie Monster

Date:

Today was sweet because...

Date:

Today was sweet because...

Date:

Today was sweet because...

SPOONFULS OF SUGAR

Date:

Today was sweet because...

_____
_____
_____

Date:

Today was sweet because...

_____
_____
_____

Date:

Today was sweet because...

_____
_____
_____

Date:

Today was sweet because...

_____
_____
_____

SPOONFULS OF SUGAR

Help pull the weeds in the yard.

"Weeds are flowers too, once you get to know them."
-A. A. Milne

Date:

Today was sweet because...

_____
_____
_____

Date:

Today was sweet because...

_____
_____
_____

Date:

Today was sweet because...

SPOONFULS OF SUGAR

Date:

Today was sweet because...

_____
_____
_____

Date:

Today was sweet because...

_____
_____
_____

Date:

Today was sweet because...

Date:

Today was sweet because...

_____
_____
_____

_____
_____
_____

SPOONFULS OF SUGAR

Donate clothes you are too big for now.

Date:

Today was sweet because...

Date:

Today was sweet because...

Date:

Today was sweet because...

SPOONFULS OF SUGAR

Date:

Today was sweet because...

_____
_____
_____

Date:

Today was sweet because...

_____
_____
_____

Date:

Today was sweet because...

Date:

Today was sweet because...

_____
_____
_____

SPOONFULS OF SUGAR

Hold the door open for the people coming in after you.

Date:

Today was sweet because...

_____
_____
_____

Date:

Today was sweet because...

_____
_____

Date:

Today was sweet because...

_____
_____

SPOONFULS OF SUGAR

Date:

Today was sweet because...

Date:

Today was sweet because...

Date:

Today was sweet because...

Date:

Today was sweet because...

SPOONFULS OF SUGAR

Draw a picture and leave it on someone's bed in your home.

Date:

Today was sweet because...

Date:

Today was sweet because...

Date:

Today was sweet because...

SPOONFULS OF SUGAR

Date:

Today was sweet because...

_____
_____
_____

Date:

Today was sweet because...

_____
_____
_____

Date:

Today was sweet because...

Date:

Today was sweet because...

_____
_____
_____

SPOONFULS OF SUGAR

Look for someone who is by themselves and sit with them!

"A smile is a friend maker."
-Bangambiki Habyarimana

Date:

Today was sweet because...

_____
_____
_____

Date:

Today was sweet because...

Date:

Today was sweet because...

SPOONFULS OF SUGAR

Date:

Today was sweet because...

_____
_____
_____
_____

Date:

Today was sweet because...

_____
_____
_____
_____

Date:

Today was sweet because...

_____
_____
_____

Date:

Today was sweet because...

_____
_____
_____

SPOONFULS OF SUGAR

Ask someone, "How is your day?" Then listen!

"When we are listened to, it creates us, makes us unfold and expand."
-Karl A. Menninger

Date:

Today was sweet because...

_____
_____
_____

Date:

Today was sweet because...

_____
_____

Date:

Today was sweet because...

_____
_____
_____

SPOONFULS OF SUGAR

Date:

Today was sweet because...

_____
_____
_____

Date:

Today was sweet because...

_____
_____
_____

Date:

Today was sweet because...

_____
_____
_____

Date:

Today was sweet because...

_____
_____
_____

SPOONFULS OF SUGAR

Check out your own library book. Make eye contact and say, "Thank you."

"Never help a child with a task at which he feels he can succeed."
-Maria Montessori

Date:

Today was sweet because...

Date:

Today was sweet because...

Date:

Today was sweet because...

SPOONFULS OF SUGAR

Date:

Today was sweet because...

_____
_____
_____

Date:

Today was sweet because...

_____
_____
_____

Date:

Today was sweet because...

Date:

Today was sweet because...

_____
_____

SPOONFULS OF SUGAR

When
someone is
sad, show
compassion.

"Have I done any good
in the world today?"
-Will L Thompson

Date:

Today was sweet because...

Date:

Today was sweet because...

Date:

Today was sweet because...

SPOONFULS OF SUGAR

Date:

Today was sweet because...

_____
_____
_____

Date:

Today was sweet because...

_____
_____
_____

Date:

Today was sweet because...

_____
_____
_____

Date:

Today was sweet because...

_____
_____
_____

SPOONFULS OF SUGAR

Be patient if something is going slower than you want.

"Life isn't about waiting for the storm to pass. It's about learning how to dance in the rain."
-Vivian Greene

Date:

Today was sweet because...

Date:

Today was sweet because...

Date:

Today was sweet because...

SPOONFULS OF SUGAR

Date:

Today was sweet because...

_____
_____
_____

Date:

Today was sweet because...

_____
_____
_____

Date:

Today was sweet because...

_____
_____
_____

Date:

Today was sweet because...

_____
_____
_____

SPOONFULS OF SUGAR

Remember your
manner words:
"Excuse me"
"Please?"
"Thank you!"
"May I?"

*"Respect is one of the greatest
expressions of love."*
-Miguel Angel Ruiz

Date:

Today was sweet because...

_____
_____
_____

Date:

Today was sweet because...

_____
_____

Date:

Today was sweet because...

_____
_____

SPOONFULS OF SUGAR

Date:

Today was sweet because...

_____
_____
_____

Date:

Today was sweet because...

_____
_____
_____

Date:

Today was sweet because...

_____
_____
_____

Date:

Today was sweet because...

_____
_____
_____

SPOONFULS OF SUGAR

Remember a really great day you had and tell someone about it.

"There is nothing in a caterpillar that tells you it's going to be a butterfly."
-R Buckminster Fuller

Date:

Today was sweet because...

Date:

Today was sweet because...

Date:

Today was sweet because...

SPOONFULS OF SUGAR

Date:

Today was sweet because...

Date:

Today was sweet because...

Date:

Today was sweet because...

Date:

Today was sweet because...

SPOONFULS OF SUGAR

Pick up your trash, whether inside or outside.

Date:

Today was sweet because...

Date:

Today was sweet because...

Date:

Today was sweet because...

SPOONFULS OF SUGAR

Date:

Today was sweet because...

_____
_____
_____

Date:

Today was sweet because...

_____
_____
_____

Date:

Today was sweet because...

Date:

Today was sweet because...

_____
_____
_____

SPOONFULS OF SUGAR

Give someone a thumbs up! Or two!

Date:

Today was sweet because...

Date:

Today was sweet because...

Date:

Today was sweet because...

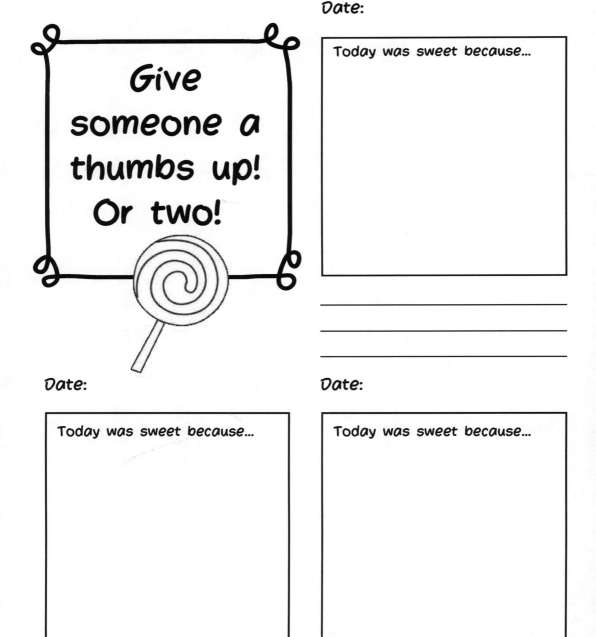

SPOONFULS OF SUGAR

Date:

Today was sweet because...

Date:

Today was sweet because...

Date:

Today was sweet because...

Date:

Today was sweet because...

SPOONFULS OF SUGAR

When you are doing something awesome, invite someone else to join in!

Date:

Today was sweet because...

Date:

Today was sweet because...

Date:

Today was sweet because...

SPOONFULS OF SUGAR

Date:

Today was sweet because...

_____
_____
_____

Date:

Today was sweet because...

_____
_____
_____

Date:

Today was sweet because...

Date:

Today was sweet because...

_____
_____
_____

SPOONFULS OF SUGAR

If you hurt someone, even on accident, be quick to say sorry!

"Never let a problem to be solved become more important than a person to be loved."
-Thomas S Monson

Date:

Today was sweet because...

Date:

Today was sweet because...

Date:

Today was sweet because...

SPOONFULS OF SUGAR

Date:

Today was sweet because...

_____
_____
_____

Date:

Today was sweet because...

_____
_____
_____

Date:

Today was sweet because...

_____
_____

Date:

Today was sweet because...

_____
_____

SPOONFULS OF SUGAR

Choose to be happy, even when you don't feel like it!

"Happiness isn't something that depends on our surroundings, it's something we make inside ourselves."
-Corrie Ten Boom

Date:

Today was sweet because...

Date:

Today was sweet because...

Date:

Today was sweet because...

SPOONFULS OF SUGAR

Date:

Today was sweet because...

_____
_____
_____

Date:

Today was sweet because...

_____
_____
_____

Date:

Today was sweet because...

_____
_____

Date:

Today was sweet because...

_____
_____

Made in the USA
Columbia, SC
07 May 2024

35323133R00052